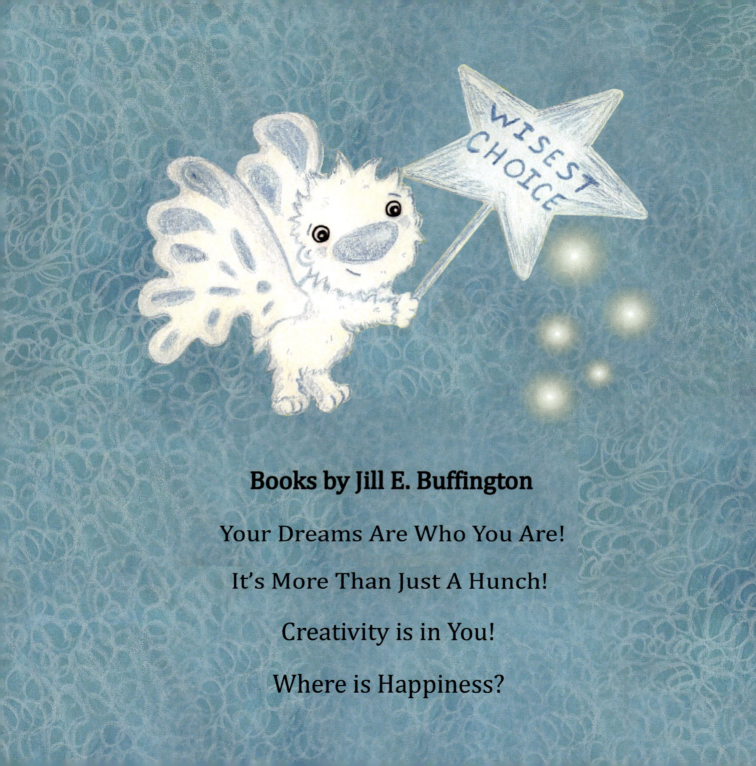

Books by Jill E. Buffington

Your Dreams Are Who You Are!

It's More Than Just A Hunch!

Creativity is in You!

Where is Happiness?

It's More Than Just a Hunch!
Copyright © 2022 by Jill Elisabeth Buffington
Registration #: TXu 2-341-242

Text and Illustrations by Jill E. Buffington
All rights reserved
ISBN: 978-1-955092-02-9

Roaring Light Productions
Somerset, MA 02726
www.jubibooks.com

Printed in the United States of America. No part of this publication may be reproduced or transmitted in any form by any means, graphic, electronic, or mechanical, including photocopying, recording, taping or any information storage or retrieval system, without permission in writing from the publisher.

Dedication

This series is dedicated to my Grandma, Janice Buffington, who gave me the artistic tools and the inspiration to be creative at a very young age. She always provided constructive criticism, constant support and encouragement. Grandma Buffington critiqued all of these illustrations at the age of 95 and passed on a few months later. She will always be my biggest fan.

Special Appreciation

Thank you to my parents, Susan and Rick Buffington who have showered me with love and support my entire life. You have both nurtured all of the creative energies I had as a child, and I am blessed to have your continued support as an adult.

Thank you to the rest of my loving family and friends who have heard about my books for years. Your excitement and support ignited my desire to share Jubi with the world!

It's More Than Just a Hunch!

By: Jill E. Buffington

Intuition is the inner voice that dwells within your spirit.

You'll need to understand a bit more in order to truly hear it.

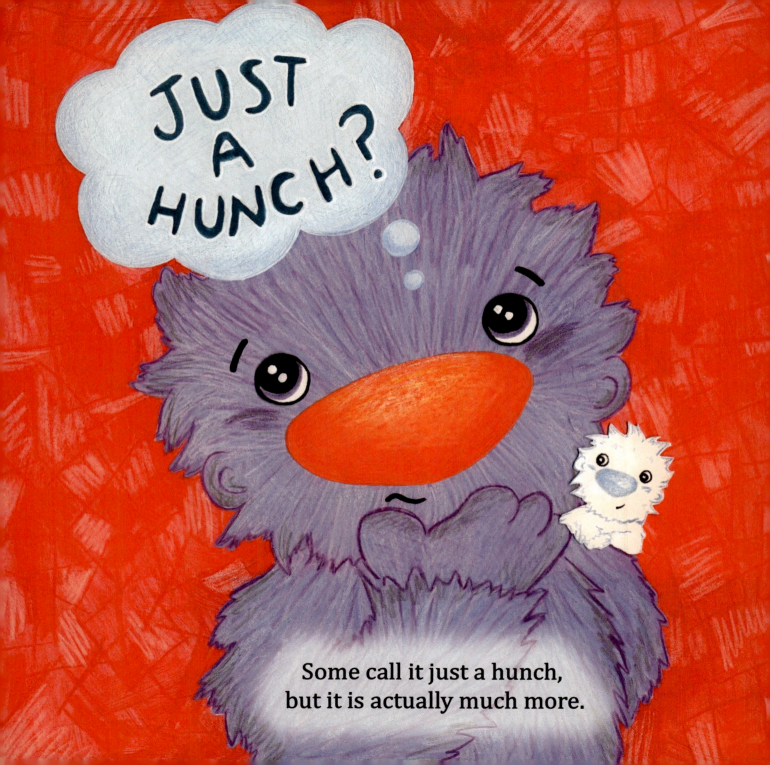

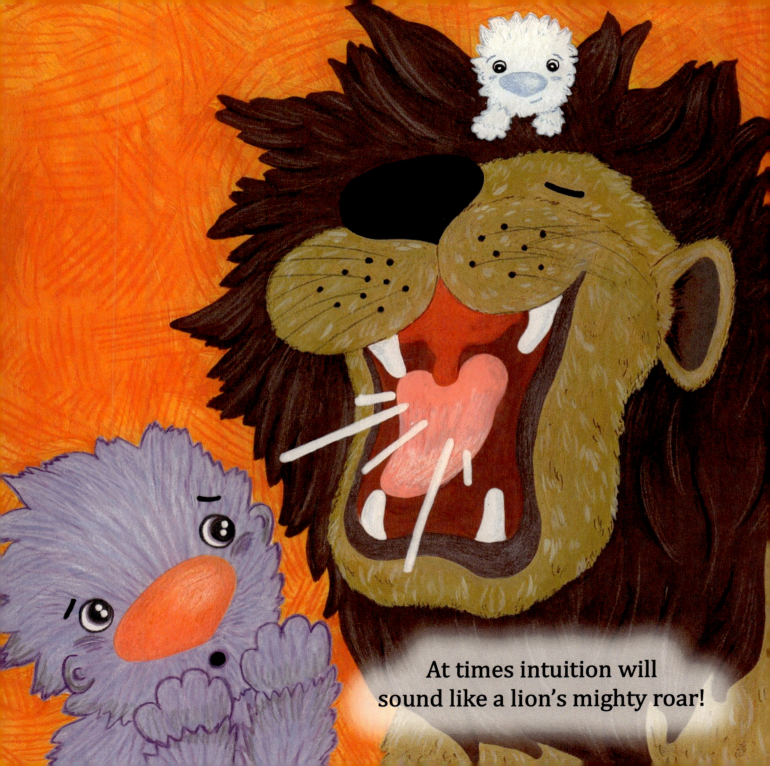

At times intuition will sound like a lion's mighty roar!

Quiet it may sound, but pay attention to where it comes from.

It's a power that will lead you to make the wisest choice,

as long as you trust and listen to this inner voice.

Your intuition will live with you throughout your entire life.

When you are slow to speak, and careful to react,

you'll be able to allow your intuition some time to act.

Intuition is a guide that shows you right from wrong.

It will also let you know when something does or doesn't belong.

That alarm can suddenly sound from deep inside your gut.

Well, that's your intuition you hear, and it's speaking only to you.

It's your first sense that you should always embrace.

Your intuition is yours; it can really change you!

It will be there all the time, whether you're happy or feeling blue.

It's so important to stay mindful of this blessing you possess.

When you're in need of guidance, just wait...
and let your intuition do the rest.

About the Author

Jill Buffington, who was born and raised in New England, lives in a cottage by the ocean with her sweet puppy Dreyfus, and curious kitties, Shamu, Hefner and Gideon. She enjoys snowy and creative winters, and fun-filled beach days in the summer. Jill's first art teacher and the most encouraging person in her artistic journey was her grandmother, who was an artist herself. "My grandmother instilled a strong artistic foundation, as well as many of the creative inspirations I use today." Jill's artistic work includes a combination of residential and commercial paintings, sculptures, book illustrations and jewelry. She has also been a part of community art healing projects across the country.

Jill has also worked in the personal and spiritual development world for over a decade. Her children's book concepts support social-emotional learning by encouraging children to be creative, trust their intuition, choose happiness, and pursue their dreams.

During the illustration process of these books, Jill was excited to use bright colors and whimsical themes. Her fun-loving and furry character "Jubi" (short for "Jubilee") was created so that children can join in with his spirited, child-like wonder while reading the series. "I've always been a creator, almost from the time I could walk. My love of art and my spiritual journey influenced this series." Jill hopes that the vibrant art and heart-felt messages will become an inspiring and meaningful part of all children's lives.

Made in the USA
Middletown, DE
26 July 2023